Kisses at the espresso bar
ekphrastic prose poems

Kisses at the espresso bar
ekphrastic prose poems

Anita Nahal

© 2022 Anita Nahal. All rights reserved.
This material may not be reproduced in any form, published,
reprinted, recorded, performed, broadcast,
rewritten or redistributed without
the explicit permission of Anita Nahal.
All such actions are strictly prohibited by law.

Cover design by Shay Culligan
Cover image by Anthony Gartmond,
graphite pencil artist, New Jersey, USA

ISBN: 978-1-63980-181-7

Kelsay Books
502 South 1040 East, A-119
American Fork, Utah 84003
Kelsaybooks.com

To my blessing, my son Vikrant, who is my constant companion and support in all my life's journeys, keeping me loved, protected, and grounded.

In the warm memory of my parents,
Drs. Chaman and Sudarshna Nahal,
for wonderous and valuable life
lessons.

To the amazing artists in this book for
their generosity in letting me run with
their artwork and creating poems
which expanded my own horizons.
Without them, my poems in this
volume would not be.

Acknowledgments

15 Contemporary Indian Poets Writing in English Anthology (2022): "Greatest warrior is metamorphic Mother Earth," "I interpret my colorless drink"

Cathexis Northwest Press: "Draupadi & Kunti" (previous title: "Of in-law daughters and mothers"), "Prayer," "Humdrum of my fabric," "Humans and extinctions"

Confluence: "Native," "Jazz Vocalist"

Das Literarisch: "Koala and Judases," "Flame and escape," "Humans and extinctions"

FemAsia: "I interpret my colorless drink," "Kisses at the espresso Bar" (previous title: "No real pleasure in the sip"), "Tears can come anytime" (previous title: "Tears")

Kaleidoscope anthology: "Love or in love," "Have and have nots," "What's up," "Can surrealism be a bench?," "Singing and lingering seven-year itches"

Pen-In-Hand: "Half woman, half empty," "Of rainbows and jelly fish"

Poetryspective: "The eyes of valentine"

Teesta Review: "Life," "Muse of biorhythms"

The Dillydoun Review: "Greatest warrior is metamorphic Mother Earth," "My Trojan horse" (previous title: "The Trojan horse"), "Whispers," "I want a wholesome life," "My soul sits at the edge of Arlington and Washington DC"

The Ekphrastic Review: "A New Day," "The eyes of valentine," "Not really like Mona Lisa" (previous title: "Sumair"), "No clean slate with blood," "Eye of the storm"

The Journal of Expressive Writing: "Ask me your fortune if you dare!"

Visual Verse: "Nagini, that may not comply," "Two wells"

What's wrong with us Kali women?: "Greatest warrior is metamorphic Mother Earth," "Koala and Judases," "I interpret my colorless drink," "Jazz vocalist," "Art gallery prediction," "Educated or enlightened," "Flame and escape," "My Trojan Horse," and "Native" (These appeared in slightly different forms in the author's third book and also in different journals as indicated in the acknowledgments.)

YapanChitra: "The eye of the storm," "The Middle Path," "If Earth had not been a mother?," "Child's game"

The pencil drawing of the image for the poem "The eyes of valentine," was created at: online.rapidresizer.com/photograph-to-pattern.php

Author's note: The author generally revises her poems long after she writes them and long after these are first published. That's the only way she believes she can improve on her writings. Therefore, you might find some of the previously published poems in this volume have been revised.

Preface

The word e*kphrastic* comes from the Greek word ekphrasis. According to the Poetry Foundation, "An ekphrastic poem is a vivid description of a scene or, more commonly, a work of art. Through the imaginative act of narrating and reflecting on the "action" of a painting or sculpture, the poet may amplify and expand its meaning." Being a visual learner, I hold a deep fascination in creating poetry with art. In my second book of poetry, *Hey, Spilt milk is spilt, nothing else* (2018), I included a pencil line recreation of pictures on almost each page. Therefore, writing ekphratic poems seemed a natural outcome.

In each poem, in this book, I have seeped in contemporary, historical, cultural, and literary nuances from different parts of the world, even inculcating some diverse language terminologies. The poems in this volume are like pieces of artwork representative of the real-surreal layered world in which we reside. Baring the image employed for first poem which is from my personal collection, this book contains images by seven artists from around the world. These include Lorette C. Luzajic, Elizabeth 'Lish' Škec, Madan Tashi, Madhumita Sinha, Michael D. Harris, Manju Narain and Anthony Gartmond. They are mixed media artists, sculptors, painters, quilt artists, visual artists, and graphite pencil artists respectively though some work on more than one medium. Their artwork is striking, intriguing, surrealist, postmodern, and hyperrealist. They inspired me, expanding my horizons vastly for which I am very thankful.

The thirty-eight poems that go with the images in the book are an abounding testament to the myriad personal and universal emotions, feelings, and perspectives I hold close to my heart and spirit. I hope the poems in this volume will take the readers on an immersive, meditative, and narrative journey, creating and recreating scenes as tremendous soulful food for thought. Most of the poems are surrealist, with reference to works of Méret Oppenheim, Salvador Dali, René Magritte, Man Ray, Giorgio de Chirico, Yves Tanguy, Amrita Sher-Gil, and Frida Kahlo. Thematically, the poems present poetic questioning and deliberations on injustice, love, rejection, conceit, life, motherhood, environment, and gender bias, among others. Like John Keats *Ode on a Grecian Urn*, in some of the poems, I speak to the objects, giving them a direct voice.

I decided on *Kisses at the espresso bar* as the title as it drew up memories of growing up in New Delhi, India. While tea is my personal favorite, as a teenager and later as a young college professor, I often accompanied my parents to fashionable restaurants in the iconic central shopping plaza, Connaught Place, where espresso was a coffee frothed to the top with light foam, variously referred to as cappuccino elsewhere in the world. That feathery tan appearance, that rich taste served in classic thick saucer and cup stayed with me and the graphite pencil line drawing by Anthony Gartmond brought forth nostalgia. I believe life is pretty much like a coffee shop. Sipping on moments, reminiscing, catching up, sharing sometimes flippant or intimate details of our lives with strangers, bonding deeply with some, reflecting upon and participating in the sadness or joy of others, and ultimately moving on with an upbeat step . . . like what coffee, or tea, brings for us.

In all my poetry books, I have pulled from my Indian birth and experience and added those from my experience in the US, my adopted land, and from countries I have visited around the world. The diaspora, the East and the West all come together with a greater focus on universality of sentiments and expressions in this book. I hope this book will become one more loved charm in your classic collection of poetry books urging you to return to my poems again and again.

—Anita Nahal

Contents

The eyes of valentine	13
Mixed Media Art by Lorette C. Luzajic	15
Nagini that may not comply	17
Eye of the storm	19
My *Trojan* horse	21
Of rainbows and jellyfish	23
A new day	25
Humans and extinctions	27
Art gallery prediction	29
I want a wholesome life	31
Ask me your fortune if you dare!	33
Love or in love?	35
No clean slate with blood	37
Native	39
Sculptures & Paintings by Elizabeth 'Lish' Škec	41
Greatest warrior is metamorphic Mother Earth	43
Educated or enlightened	45
Half woman, half-empty	47
Koala and *Judases*	49
Draupadi and *Kunti*	51
Thangka & Mandala Paintings by Madan Tashi	53
The Middle Path	55
If Earth had not been a mother?	57

Paintings by Madhumita Sinha	59
Flame and escape	61
Prayer	63
Visual & Mixed Media Art by Michael D. Harris	64
Haves and have nots	67
Humdrum of my fabric	69
What's up?	71
Quilt Art by Manju Narain	73
Life	75
Muse of biorhythms	77
Graphite Pencil Art by Anthony Gartmond	78
I interpret my colorless drink	81
Child's game	83
Kisses at the espresso bar	85
Two wells	87
Jazz vocalist	89
My soul sits at the edge of Arlington and Washington DC	91
Can surrealism be a bench?	93
Not really like *Mona Lisa*	95
Tears can come anytime	97
Singing and lingering seven-year itches	99
Whispers	101
About the Author	103

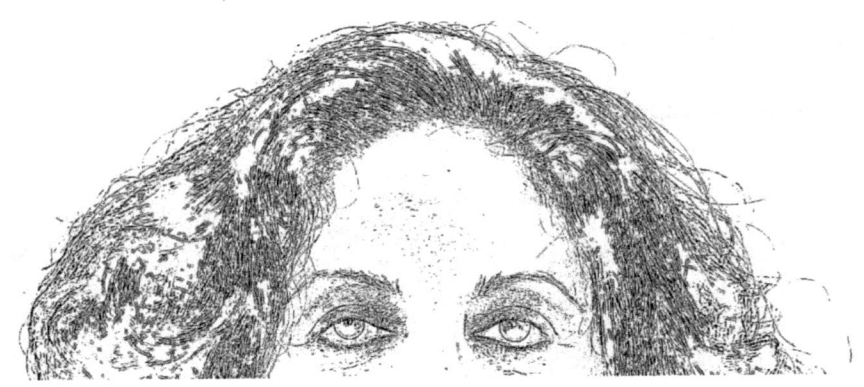

From the author's personal collection

The eyes of valentine

Eyes are generally wise. Lived eons flying on ancient prayers. Lived with you. In you. With me. In me. And outside like old sages. Their knotted pignut hickory walking sticks snoring on their side, knowing more than them. The curve, the slant, the paint brushes the eyes hold. The shivers that smolder in cold winter icy winds. The red air that quivers like *loos* of grave summer India. Or could be anywhere. *Loos* whistle and scream like over boiled tea kettles or like pensive, pinning storms hitting the buttons of my shirt hugging me lose. Clasping of my hands, I can see. The hands of the eyes that I can feel. Feel the stance. The slight bent at the corner of the eye's rump. The pimples are bursting carbonations of purple. Purple that turns into my hair dancing wild with sea horses on the beach. Goldfishes lay in pink hearts, singing. Their fins play on piano keys hanging from their backs on hooks stainless steel polished. The sky is unflappable. Not bothered. I am bothered when my eyes look into yours and your head walks away on two empty legs. I can hear the sky cringing. I become a pair of new ballet shoes yearning for love and wisdom. *Saraswati* is nearby. *Shiva* is not far away. Yin and yang sit on my eyelids. I fly out to the ocean, composed, collected, in a plethora of perceptive, wispy blues, flamingo pinks and satin peach hues. A hunched sky full of humans' secrets, joins me. Much learning is still to be done.

*Valentine: Valentine's Day, also called Saint Valentine's Day, is celebrated annually on February 14 *Loos: Hot winds *Saraswati: Hindu goddess of knowledge, wisdom, learning and creativity *Shiva: Hindu god, one of the three in the Trinity of Hindu gods. Shiva is known as the destroyer.

Mixed Media Art by Lorette C. Luzajic
Toronto, Canada

Lorette C. Luzajic is the founding editor of *The Ekphrastic Review,* a journal devoted to literature inspired by visual art. Her prose poetry and small stories have been published widely in *Ghost Parachute, Tiny Molecules, MacQueen's Quarterly, The Dillydoun Review, Indelible, Cleaver, Flash Boulevard,* and *Unbroken Journal,* along with many anthologies. Lorette is also an internationally celebrated visual artist who works in mixed media and collage.

Anita came to know Lorette when some of her poems found a home in the creatively inquisitive, *The Ekphrastic Review*. Little did she realize at the time that Lorette was herself not only a poet but also an incredible mixed media artist who created spectacular visuals combining myriad art forms. Lorette's art pieces have been described as, "A superhuman effort to coalesce the imaginative world" by Moray Mair, *Mutant Space Arts*. For more on Lorette, please visit: https://www.mixedupmedia.ca/

Wild Thing 12"x12", mixed media on canvas

Nagini that may not comply

The umbilical cord, the incense that heralds new birth, the smoke that rises from *handi* labored sustenance, the fumes above a pyre, someone's tail scampering off into the thick . . . all turns and twists of creation, celebration, destruction that I can recite in ballads of kingdoms underground, overground, guarded by *Nehebkau* or by *Jatakas*, or *Sita*'s heart set on a fake deer, and commoners roaming around animated. Things were not always under control . . . just beneath the surface. I can recite a limerick to lighten the mood.
Once upon a time a serpent lived across the moat/He had a beard like that of a goat/The goat he ate/His own beard was the bait/The serpent who lived across the moat.
Does it help? *Nummo, Nagas, Cernunnos,* all avatars are intertwined with humanity. Humanity which portends good, bad, evil. The she and he, and everyone else. Antlers, birds, and fish pass by scribbling graffiti. Graffiti of lives gentrified. Free falling with odd meteors in a tormented pale sky. And the handler with his one foot cramped against the neck, forcing a predicted outcome has humankind aghast with mouths gaping, lips pouting, eyes crestfallen, steamy, yet quizzing. Some unbeknownst hands create illegible alphabet patterns in the dirt like escape routes out the maze, reminding life is in our hands. Don't blame mythologies and reincarnations. Don't be fooled by stories you did not write or witness. Don't write stories of destruction to give a pass to the rider. Don't then bid the *Nagini* to the sacrifice. Do you think she will comply?

---

*Nagini: Hindi word for female snake *Handi: Hindi word for a cooking utensil made of copper or clay *Nehebkau: Snake god in ancient Egyptian mythology *Jatakas: Tales of the Buddha's past lives. The Pali Jatakas record 357 past lives as a human, 66 as a god, and 123 as an animal *Nummo: Ancestral spirits among the Dogon people of Mali *Naga: Hindi word for the male snake/superhuman spirit in snake shape *Cernunnos: Horned Celtic god of the animals

Fundamental Pictures 24"x24", mixed media on gallery canvas

Eye of the storm

Sometimes I sit at its periphery. Quite singular. Floating around are lazy *cockatoo wasp fish*. So lazy, so lazy, mistaken for dead leaves. *Feuille morte!* Charlotte Brontë got me with, *"I found no pleasure in the silent trees, the falling fir-cones, the congealed relics of autumn, russet leaves, swept by past winds in heaps, and now stiffened together."* I wipe the irk from the corner of the eye which keeps flickering. I pry it open to check for any further rankle or two wedged or floating somewhere . . . tiny fibers in the *vitreous humor*. A mining torch strapped to my forehead beams direct. Sometimes if a deeper cleaning is obligatory or indispensable, I step inside in rain boots lest the *aqueous humor* in the assembly line is in overtime. *Toofans* kind of have that reputation. Like ones inside unpretentious hearts, uncrowded minds. My periscope is always handy in case I get pulled into another attribute where the eye rubbernecks at me and the squall is kind of nameless, undefined, unrefined. This eye is unusual, can't see with it, can't place it in a face, can't gift it to anyone, can't take it off, can't let it have time out even in an open pandora's box. It keeps steady at 15–20 blinks per minute. Disturbing. Annoying. Flirting. All but sleeping. Unlike the blissful calm of boats docked in a row at a marina at dawn.

*Feuille Morte: French for dead leaf *Charlotte Brontë: *Jane Eyre*, 1847 *Vitreous humor: A colorless, transparent, gel-like substance that fills the space between the lens and the retina within the eye *Aqueous humor: A clear liquid in the front of the eye *Toofan: Hindi word for storm

Are You a Figment of My Imagination, or Am I a Figment of Yours? 24"x24", mixed media on gallery canvas

My *Trojan* horse

Yes, we let our ego be center stage on occasions, and my ego became the *Trojan* horse. I, myself, constructed the *Gulliverian* prop, then willingly revealed the path to the sanctity of my comprehensions. It proved treacherous. I alerted my conscience that I wanted to be found hastily. Other horses standing at the flanks, joined my *Trojan* with necks twisted, eyes massive and bolting, legs twined, tails growing from navels, mouths leering, hooves puffing, manes stiff like frightened quills fallen off a porcupine. Few human faces focus on the fight, unnerved . . . rest are barren, nonchalant. As my *Trojan* fell on its back, the bulls came darting poised for the final denunciation. I upturned my hands to face the sky seeking alms of forgiveness. The bulls transformed into thousands of *Ganesha*, some airborne, some prancing, one sitting right near me. Engrossed. Observing my manifestations. I was able to walk away, ego bruised, subdued, ready to start anew. That night I pushed my *Trojan* into *Ganesha*'s care to be melted and reused as asphalt binding me to modesty.

*Trojan horse: Refers to a wooden horse used by the Greeks in the Trojan war
*Gulliverian: Reference to Gulliver's Travels by Jonathan Swift *Ganesha: Hindu God of prosperity and good luck

Red and White Blues, 48"x 36", mixed media on gallery canvas

Of rainbows and jellyfish

My soul has batik splatters of favored hues of carrot, baby powder, kale, mustard, crimson, and pistachio. I can munch on most feeling healthy, splash some powder to feel cool, and sit on a block bench to feel organic. I use adjusted length pencils with erasers for ready reference. Need can arise anytime to wade with the flow. Scripts have been angling and yearning. Angling and yearning for scores and scores for a rainbow to come waving ever so gently, lest destiny scares it away. And I see my black chiffon bikini peeking from beneath my gold satin embroidered sarong as I lay on a stripped red and white, candy cane beach towel sipping fruity cocktails with painted paper umbrellas popping out, flirting with the smooth, suave breeze. I am old enough now to wear a bikini to the chagrin of many. My soul joins the teasing with verses, strokes, brushes, and daydreams. Amused jellyfish bounce way out the ocean, shrieking and chortling like little children watching a nondescript bio-scope show. The afternoon winter sun urges me to catnap, take it easy, let them be. On waking slightly, I find cherry, slate, sapphire, coffee, and silver jellyfish sauntering, napping side by side with me on the malleable sand. Paper umbrellas from my cocktail have jumped purpose providing them welcomed shade and I am beginning to tan more and more. Didn't think a brown girl could tan. #browngirlscantan. My parents' vintage *gramophone* is blaring eclectic tunes when finally, a rain-bowed soul knocks on my head. I awaken fully and walk over with clear lens to the dance party now in full swing.

---

*Gramophone: The first gramophone with grooves interpreted on flat discs was invented by German American Emile Berliner in 1887

Corona Planet, 12"x12", mixed media on canvas

A new day

Clap, clap, clap. The sky is ablaze with lighted hands clapping. An equal number of feet join the prance. There is no need for radio or television. Covid19 seems trapped in some bubbles, circles, abstracts. Everywhere else tranquility seems to prevail. I finally go out wearing gold sheer stilettoes, a wrap skirt in metallic, wrist choker gilded too, orange gloss on my lips. I see drizzle dripping cars drive by. Cars are circles. Buildings are slender, straight into the ground or nowhere. Indigo grass is growing on thin lengths of reed. Chewing gum mouths move noisily. Tongues are florescent. Many hued shops and neon signs gesture with a forefinger pointing at us from restaurant tops. Rest is hidden, cut by huge scissors that hang from the sky. I see you and me as two shadows between the ridges. Ache to touch. The music is loud. You are not there in flesh to tango with me. I am alone in all the wet circles and keep swirling like *dervishes* in a trance seemingly going on forever. I run helter-skelter, opening all the doors till I see my bed neat and ready. I don't waste time. Let no haunts visit my dreams either. Next morning is fresh like a newly plucked tangerine. As I sip the juice, the phone rings. *"Corona took him."* Residue of the booster in my arm hurts but it's a new day.

*Dervishes: A member of a Muslim religious order noted for devotional exercises especially dancing in circles

A Friend Indeed, 24"x24", mixed media on gallery canvas

Humans and extinctions

The last hatchling of the *ancient great roamer* was born before humans came along to burn history. Boulders yawned with wide open mouths. Let out ecstatic, climatic, high-pitched sounds. The skies were eerily discreet with hands behind ears trying hard to decipher inaudible echoes that reverberated in the leaden, dreary, asafetida filled clouds. A kind of protracted, pungent, daunting humming could be heard miles away. Downpours were attempting to fall uniform and demonstrative, descending into new rivers being charted at the confluence of liquids, heat, oxygen, mud. And *Pleistocene* in Australia lit up as tall standing *Megalania* hit their chests, drumming the birth shower to an end as mom and fledgling watched the regalia reach its crescendo. Butterflies even tried some magic. The mom perched above the baby completing the shedding of the amniotic fluid. She perched even higher above the cacophony. Anxious and vexed, ready to pounce and gobble any extinct predators emerging from abrasions in dimensions. Her eyesight acute, fully awake, observing the humans igniting the match. Dinosaurs vanished soon after. And friendships can be easily bought.

*Pleistocene: Also referred to as the Ice Age *Ancient great roamer: Name given to the most giant terrestrial lizard, Megalania, by Richard Owen, who first wrote about them

Bye, Bye Blackbird, 12"x12", mixed media on canvas

Art gallery prediction

I'd once gone to Pittsburg on a paid sojourn as most conferences end up being. Strangers I'd just met and laughed heartily over wine and cheese accompanied me to observe the thought processes of a pop artist icon. Inside the dimly lit building, one of them held my hand, pulled me for a kiss. I exclaimed in awe at an odd projection crafted with a deck of cards and discarded sashes from carefully wrapped presents. He left with a huff. A mad world I thought. Or he thought? A stuffed crow stood by watching a sparrow sitting daintily on a heart. Was it trying to claim it surreptitiously? Was humanity going barmy? *"Caw, caw,"* was its throaty kraa call, cautioning, prophesizing like *Apollo*. Numbers and alphabets flashed in the yellow fog dominant in the maize that held its own. Not upbeat, just rigid like corn in an endless field with no breeze blowing. Scratching heads, full of lice were conjecturing for remedies to life's madness. Bob Dylan and Andy Warhol stood behind the deck of cards guessing next moves. The lice gave up, stamped out in unison and the crow began singing, *"The answer, my friend, is blowin' in the wind/The answer is blowin' in the wind."* Plops of paint dripped from cleverly laid brushes resplendent with matte color and an old *Olivetti* had garbled letters typed on plain paper with stencil cut outs laying on their backs. Balloons of unalike shapes had caught the dripping paint. Stuffing their tummies, they grumbled of feeling bloated and bouncy. The exhibit was titled, *A mad world to be.*

*Apollo: Greek God of music, poetry, and a heralder of caution and moderation *"The answer, my friend, is blowin' in the wind/The answer is blowin' in the wind," is part of Bob Dylan's song, Blowin In The Wind released in 1963 in his album, The Freewheelin *Olivetti: A typewriter designed by Marcello Nizzoli in 1948

Blame It on My Wild Heart, 12"x12", mixed media on canvas

I want a wholesome life

Which might explain why like pieces of bread dunked in hot tea or milk I may fall off abruptly without even the slightest tug. Pliable and desirous to be held without as much as a word. You'll try picking up remains metastasizing like kneaded dough gone awry, rolling like a gooey ball stuck. Stuck, stuck, refusing to budge. Not mine nor your peace wanting to smudge. A wholesome life I crave, and craving has a mind of its own, staggering behind or in eternities ahead. It's not that my heart is not beating love, not that my heart is not oozing desire, not that my heart doesn't wanna give or receive. If not, why would I be waving it as a flag then? Or place it bejeweled, blushing outside my body, then? I even carry a magician's hat tossing and revolving, conjuring spells out the *Book of Shadows*. At twenty-nine I gazed at distant stars gently urging and rubbing shoulders with them, wistfully beseeching voyages. Now stars rubbing shoulders with each other gaze at me, nodding sympathetically at the frayed knots of my virgin romances gone astray. Baggage becomes dense, worn out, yet wheels are not ready to squeak and repose. I let the pointed peep toes of yesteryears go switching to block heels instead. Shorter I appear, the shorter and shorter I become, wider and wider the distances between you and me. On many tongues sit #&'s and the #&'s increase in quantity and volume as they attempt replacing #buts. A mammoth robotic lottery wheel circles my face becoming one with partitions in my brain. Not many can keep rolling without any *moolah* coming their way.

*Book of Shadows: A book containing religious text and instructions for magical rituals found within the Neopagan religion of Wicca *Moolah: slang word for money, being employed in the poem to denote anything of value

Queen of the Woodpeckers, 12"x12", mixed media on canvas

Ask me your fortune if you dare!

Brewed slowly the good ole broth
Leisurely like the walk of a sloth
Cold was *Pythia*'s war soup
Fortune teller had no stoop
Brewed slowly the good ole broth.

Lentil or meat in a steaming hot pot
Reeked heavy and was badly sought
Remnants of birds in the ladle
Ramifications recurring without a paddle
Lentil or meat in a steaming hot pot.

Fortune teller, grumpy and displeased
As if from torture she wanted release
Omikuji seekers looked for help
Thin paper strips flew by in yelp
Fortune teller, grumpy and displeased.

Oh! The irony of hand's dealt cards
Somewhere a poet sat writing these bards
Teller in poverty
Seekers in royalty
Oh, the irony of hand's dealt cards.

*Pythia: Pythia was the name of the high priestess of the Temple of Apollo at Delphi and was its oracle *Omikuji: Paper strips with a fortune written on them at Shinto shrines and Buddhist temples in Japan

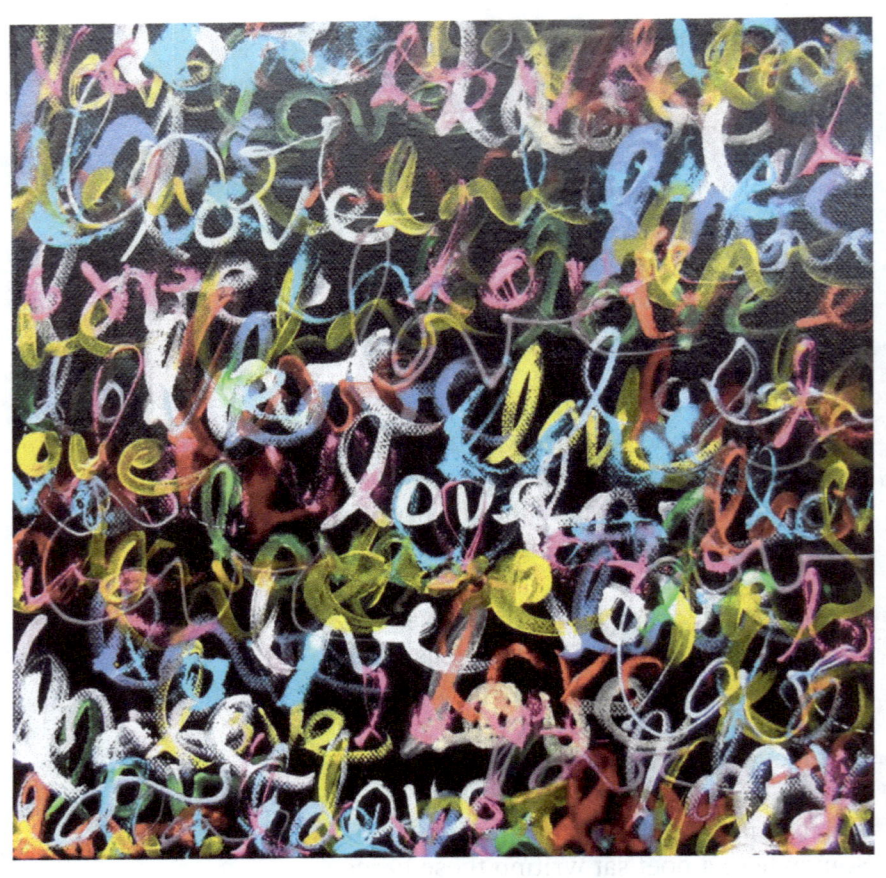

Love (rainbow), 12"x12", mixed media on canvas

Love or in love?

Can't seem to make them sit together. Without fidgeting. Without sneering. At each other. Or smirking. At me. They like to wear matching clothes throwing off desires, dreams, assumptions, deductions, operational gumptions. Twins without a joint mission. Twins without feeling emotions of the other. Twins on a rocky pendulum. One they play with telepathic neurotransmitters while their sciatica is pinching them with sharp nailed fingertips. I see a plethora of chalk boards on nimble stands fox trotting around. Some like to waltz on train stations and airports. Journeying without a destination. Journeying without a purpose. Journeying without heart. Some get stuck in pliable sand. Some poke their head above the muck. Some swim beneath the permafrost. Some become snow cones to be sucked or thrown into dust bins. Some revel in warm chocolate and strawberry *chutneys*. Some play it cool in mint sprinkled yogurt bowls. Some clasp my fingers. Some stealthily drift away as if from the other side of the moon they had a call. Cupid had flown the coop. *Sex and the City* wasn't a shy one. *"I love you, but I'm not in love with you,"* was on the lips of the walking dead T-Rex as they gobbled up you and me.

*Chutneys: A chutney is the Hindi word for condiment or sauce * Sex and the City is an American television series adaptation of Candace Bushnell's 1997 novel by the same name. *T-Rex: Short for, Tyrannosaurus

I Struggled With Words, For Fear They Would Give Me Away,
24"x24", mixed media on gallery canvas

No clean slate with blood

Let us start on a clean slate. A clean slate it will be. Will it? For whom? Victors? Losers? Departers? Anglers? Jigsaw puzzle of spoils remains incomplete. Truth, dare, brinkmanship, all consummating. Horrific orgy of breaths and breathing. Life. Death. Exhumed. Everyone is scattering us. Our emotions, beliefs, roots, bones, blood, longings, belongings, family, friends, futures. Petitions gone into hiding. Or lost. Or bon-fired. Pushing. Stampeding. Wedging. Transporting. Not knowing where we're going. Knowing only, we're grabbing something that smells of freedom. What will I write when the slate has been washed, blood mopped, tears dried? When screams and pleas have been chock-held? Drowned? Will I feel like writing then? With my innocent children muffled. With my parents left standing on a frenzied tarmac as plane doors padlocked. I was the last allowed to board, huddled maskless next to strangers. My heart served on a privileged platter I did not bake, still pulsating like fish out the water. I realize now why I don't eat sea food. Crabs and lobsters thrown alive in boiling water with their stalks watching intently, petrified, yet proud with claw thumbs straight up, screaming at top of their dwindling lungs, *"I give a damn; karma doesn't take too long."* My identity, your identity, your world, my world, moving in different speeds, directions, fissures. *The Matrix* was on replay. Dystopia-he was dragging utopia-she by her hair. Primitive societies were returning, hatched in laboratories of the gluttonous in many *Jurassic* parks. And then, there was a union, a marriage of senseless squabbles of mice and men. We became a speck on the messy roll of the film for the nightly news.

*The Matrix: A 1999 science fiction action film directed by Lana Wachowski and Lilly Wachowski *Jurassic: Jurassic Park is a 1993 American science fiction action film directed by Steven Spielberg which was followed by several sequels

Pop Goes the World, 40"x40", mixed media on gallery canvas

Native

Bury My Heart at Wounded Knee was playing on a mega screen on the expansive canvas of captured fields. People were scampering around filling in the shadows of the good, bad, evil. Each side in history believes its right. Arrows, bullets, and *lacrimis* mixed with neigh of horses were lying on their side, wounded in body and pride. Blood and the guilty swarmed like hungry, disturbed bees. The pile was mile high. Rusted, tainted buggy lines had left permanent etchings in the muddied road in which *lilliputian* minds pushed their bayonets into people's shoeless feet. Far away on the pink horizon, one could hear the wolves howling, babies lachrymose, mothers wailing, and young and all lost. Bison with lush jade grass growing from their backs sit at the entrance of a burning teepee village begging to be fed and eaten like before. The railroad keeps moving. Like in *Time Transfixed,* the very thriving, real, malleable, touchable smoke appears a welcoming mirage. Or not. Penetrating through the torture and silence of the lambs. The steam is chocking up and burning inside, outside. Can you see or hear? No onomatopoeia exists for the sounds of civilizational truths and lies.

*Lacrimis: Latin for the word, tears *Lilliputian: Means a small person or thing. Its popular usage comes from Jonathan Swift's novel, Gulliver's Travels *Time Transfixed: Painting by René Magritte (1938)

Sculptures & Paintings by Elizabeth 'Lish' Škec
Melbourne, Australian

Music, poetics, theatre, sculpture, and twirling fire, Elizabeth Lish Skec, is multi-talented! She has written poetry, plays, short stories, comedy, and songs for adults and children. She has two chapbooks, *Butterflies of New Dawn* (1995) and *Leather Skin* (2002), and one recent poetry collection, *Breath,* published by Luckner Press in 2014. She's published in various anthologies worldwide. Lish has taught poetry, creative writing, and theatre workshops for The Victorian Writers Centre, CERES, Overload Poetry Festival, and SPAN Community House, and she was part of the educational video series 'Picking Poetry Apart.' Lish was the winner of the Human Rights Poetry slam in 2011. She was also one of the four founders of Accidental Poets @goodmorningcaptain. Since then, Lish has organized and hosted readings at various venues around Australia. Lish is the founder and host of the current fortnightly gig Poetryspective at Pride Of Our Footscray Community Bar and the Poetryspective program online. For more on her, please visit: https://au.linkedin.com/in/elizabeth-%C5%A1kec-3a06bbb5

Anita came to know Elizabeth on Facebook and learned about her highly original and ingenious video poetry presentations in which her poems were given a home as well. Anita kept up with Elizabeth's other marvelous talents, such as sculpting and painting, and found them eye-popping.

Greatest warrior is metamorphic Mother Earth

Petals adorn my broken self and like our ancestors I search for the yarn and fable in each. Seeking the shadows of animals that stood with us. Seeking the brothers and sisters that fought with us. The crackling of winter fires that sheltered us. Some have roamed the world, seeing, sprouting, waning, passing into elements inside us where we go when others treat us different. Don't shake your head and offer pity over my amputated legs. Ask instead, what, where, why they walked, kicked, dragged, were slumped upon. How a warrior I was born. Don't nod in understanding without looking straight into my eyes which still sparkle in my guillotined head on the butcher block. How a warrior I was reborn. Don't put your arms around mine without feeling the compacted air that extends beyond my shredded joints. How a warrior I was born, again and again and again. *Joan of Arc, Takeko, Lozen, Rani of Jhansi,* rising, falling, rising. Don't offer to cover me up with your tainted blanket. With your prude coat. With your carefully sculpted sentences pulling a spoof that you are wise. Don't smirk at distances between loves. Don't try walking on my footprint's ashes still smoldering. Don't look for my hands to grip, to tell a joint story. Don't. Don't. Just watch. Just watch as my remaining petals keep disappearing. Watch the air around you solidify. Watch the ground beneath you harden like metamorphic rocks. Watch till I become a whisper at the end of the last drop of water. And then, you can scream.

*Joan of Arc, Nakano Takeko, Lozen, Rani of Jhansi: French, Japanese, Native American, and Indian women warriors respectively

Educated or enlightened

Two miniature tango dancers are swirling in front of my eyes, in midair. So is a piece of cheesecake. My tongue tries to latch on to its delectable taste. I feel elated, and the music is subtle and promising. Perfumed flowers drift out my nose. A burly hand pulls the cake away and suddenly, some of my tears go drifting by as huge as snow globes with me inside waving frantically. I straighten, try to walk away and step into a giant moat with sticky notes swiveling like mini tornadoes. *"Forget it, we ain't gonna say sorry"* written on each one of them. They stick to my body, and I'm sucked into the vortex of minuscule grave whirlwinds twisting. Swiveling, unstoppably falling with many splashes into the moat. I slip into intense sleep. I can still hear some men and women standing on the water promoting big authors and impressionism, existentialism, surrealism, telling me they are sharing their education. Then they turn around, running away fast, hooting, almost splitting when their hilarity reaches their belly sack's inner membranes. I can see mushy tissues, skin and veins shaking, almost coughing. A giant, cracked incandescent bulb runs after them with me on its heels close behind tugging at the on-off switch. On-off, on-off, on-off. Education zooms. Sits high on sooty clouds while enlightenment creates a new world in earth, fire, water, wind, and ether. The bulb keeps going on-off, on-off, on-off in both worlds, lest either forget. Bemused, *Thomas Edison* sits in *Sukhasana*.

---

*Sukhasana: A yogic pose in which the body sits cross-legged

Half woman, half-empty

Half woman, half empty. Or so they say. Meditating on top of the Himalayas. Proletariat, bourgeoise, and *Dalai Lamas* from generations past congregate to break bread. The other half is nurturing, soothing, preparing the planet for *Shangri-La*. A hefty, viscous, operose task. Driven by sheer power like *Jaegers* from *Pacific Rim*. Driven by wisdom marinated like mama's pickles maturing in the hot sun. Driven by aches and pains of sockets waning and unoiled. Driven by sounds. Tons and tons of sounds, even from ribbed, mocking, eerie lights inverted in *René Magritte's The Empire of Lights*. Sounds topsy turning the weighing scale. Rooms, streets, very air we inhale, replete with sounds. Sounds ticking. Sounds hiking. Sounds screeching. Sounds treading. Sounds hovering above dense snows or lying camouflaged among coral reefs. *Gala* lay unsuspecting as mismatched nesting attackers hovered for the kill. They weren't sweet. Would've been more than a bee sting. Susurrus of half woman, half empty, proletariat, bourgeoise and *Dalai Lamas*, tries to soar. Words are seen coming out as letters from mouths only to slide back when hands hoist in caution. The *Elysium fields* are not as smooth or idyllic as most dream and clearly hierarchical. Need taming, some men say, like *Shakespeare*'s shrew. Congregation ends. Half woman returns home to the other half, repeating confidently, *"She's not, they're not, I'm not, you're not, half empty. Still in the making till we pass into our next birth. A bit more made. We'll never know and begin again as half trying to be full."* Why is becoming full a gendered thing? Blimey!

---

*Shangri-La: A fictional, harmonious place first described by British author James Hilton in his 1933 novel, Lost Horizon *Jaegers from Pacific Rim: Building-sized machines piloted by humans in the 2013 American Sci-fi movie, Pacific Rim *The Empire of Lights, a 1954 painting by René Magritte *Gala: Believed to be Salvador Dali's muse and lover *Elysium Fields: Beautiful underworld meadows from Greek mythology

Koala and *Judases*

Mean, mean people slowly unwrap like sundry skins. I welcomed them so I hold culpability. They slither away leaving me to create, tend, love, rear a new skin, over and over. *Judases*. The forest is desiccated, fragile. Perfect for a fire. I don't smoke. But I see your smoky footprints in my backyard, sore and fiery, leaving me to douse these with my own skin, my own fabrics, my own rush, over and over. *Judases*. Ghosts of the *Amazonia, Dering woods, Crooked Forest,* the *Tsingy,* the *Black Forest,* the *Tongass,* the *Sundarbans* and myriad more let out *banshee* screams often. See my skin, my bark, my leaves, my tiny legs heaped in layers on the sun's anchor. *Judases*. I see wisdom knocking on my door, solidly, repetitively. I see the residues from rampant wildfires spill just outside my abode. I see you and others cooking on those very dangerous embers. *Judases*. I don't watch. I observe. I look pointedly. That's my job. Like the Gods of all religions observing us. I may look short and cute, yet I thrive on tall Eucalyptus that your pettiness can never reach, unless you burn the trees. I can live long except for your foolhardiness that lights a match or pulls along in old, smelly rags your diseases with the intent to devastate, kill. I'm forced to be your sins. Your narcissism. Your juvenile behavior protruding like *Pinocchio*'s nose. *Judases*.

*Judases: One who betrays another in the cloak of friendship *Amazonia: Amazon rainforest *Dering woods: Kent, England *Crooked Forest: West Pomerania, Poland *Tsingy: De Bemaraha district, Madagascar *The Black Forest: Baden-Wurttemberg, Germany *Tongass: Southeast Alaska *Sundarbans: West Bengal, India, and Southern Bangladesh *Banshee: From the Irish folklore, she is a female spirit heralding the death of a family member *Pinocchio: Children's story originally written by Italian writer, Carlo Collodi

Draupadi and *Kunti*

And so *Draupadi*'s bridal sari was ensconced in a monsoon drizzle of wishful sequins that came sauntering carrying whispers of celebrations and warnings. Like a flag of defiance, she held her sari *pallu* high. Bedazzles of a neoteric doomed marriage could be heard in the vicinity of the cloaked moon and human eyes were seen grandiose and lowered resting on human head apexes. *Draupadi*'s strides irreverential to the glass of norms and respect her mother-in-law, *Kunti,* gave her who perhaps said, *"Drink it up, its hot outside, and you have to satisfy all five of my sons."* The glass fell, rolled off into a painting a non-ally was drawing. Inside the canvas nail splinters became flying feathers, searching for their throbs gone too soon. Colored strokes became rivers and canals and veins and arteries. Parts of the brain seemed missing or heralding a distinctive era with assorted drawers opening and slamming shut much to the chagrin of odd mechanical women in *Dali*'s *Burning Giraffe*. Was he mocking? *Draupadi*'s amusement and caution were seen shaking hands, clumsily, dreadfully, rebelliously. Water lay comatose watching from within a pottery urn sitting cross-legged inside *Draupadi*'s esophagus. Frosty. Undrunk. Unfelt. Unquenched thirst like the unseen itch of ageless conifer trees, like the hallowed belching of rainbowed sun laved skies, like the hysterical land beneath a fatigued dam of quicksand. *Draupadi* was fine gold dust out the time glass. There was no going back and henceforth when she spoke, her body slid through sandglass's tapered waist reappearing as disillusioned morsels of scalding boiled rice which she trundled the same for everyone.

*Draupadi: Heroine of the Hindu epic, Mahabharata *Kunti: Mother of the Pandavas and Draupadi's mother-in-law in Mahabharata *Pallu: End of the Indian attire, Sari *Burning Giraffe: Painted in 1937 by Salvador Dali

Thangka & Mandala Paintings by Madan Tashi,
a Garhwali artist, Mussoorie, India

Madan Tashi lives in a Tibetan refugee village in Mussoorie, Uttarakhand called "Happy Valley." It's a close-knit community that dates to 1954 when Tibetans were forced to flee their native homeland. Born in 1957, Madan has traveled to Tibet a few times, but his life was in peril. He is a Thangka painter by profession and devoted to Buddhist sacred art. He has painted several murals in the "Mindrolling Stupa" in Dehradun, Uttarakhand, and in the local temples in Mussoorie. Lately, he has been painting at the Ithaca Home Forests in Mussoorie on the walls of a Nature Cathedral. His art is described as "remarkable and needing global attention" by Anu Kumar, a naturalist, mindful practitioner, and supporter of pashmina weaving and local artists in Mussoorie, India. Anu Kumar introduced Madan's fabulous art to Anita.

The Middle Path

Evolving humans often lurk in *Buddha*'s *Middle Path*. Eyes downcast, not open or daunting, taunting like those of *Himalayan* tigers on the hunt for food, hunger, thirst, trampolining humanity from its malaise or simply surviving. Stop enroaching they shout! Sins of self, others, keep seekers awake at night rummaging the alleys of Buddha's steps for some learning, some salvation, some morsels. *Anne Frank* poured her prayers in *Het Achterhuis-the house behind* without any lifespan deliverances. Teeth barred, the tiger's eyes riveting in darkness are startling. I could hear many grown boots and baby shoes going somewhere, not sure where. They sounded urgent. Somewhere in the midpoint the two were trying to balance the scales. The stripped-on-orange stood majestic in stance and strides. *"Shall I eat you?"* *Darwin* and *Herbert Spencer* might be tossing in their graves, slapping themselves at the moronic intelligence of humans. The fittest survive had been their town crier pronouncements for long, history for sure on their side, while humans slept proud and gullible in each other's arms relishing borrowed crumbs of normal life. It's calm in the boscage as of now. Pastels join the verdure in trees and streams of propitious light circulate in azure waters. Clairvoyant phosphorescent eyes expand in sheer caution in the tiger's face. Connecting with my soul. With your soul. Their soul. Planet's soul. Life's soul. Souls with souls, even those departed. Seems like it's *The Last Supper*.

*Buddha's Middle Path: Propagates achieving a middle balance between extremes in emotions and action *Het Achterhuis: The house behind: A secret door led to another part of the house, an annex, where Anne Frank and her family hid during the Nazi occupation of The Netherlands *The Last Supper: In the Bible, it was the last meal Jesus ate with his disciples before his betrayal and arrest

If Earth had not been a mother?

Would it have been pilferaged? A gigantic question in *Bitter Leaf* is nailed to the wall of the roped sky. Respond please. If the felines had not guarded the gates to the tubers, would the howls and barks been different? Respond please. What about the birds, foxes, dogs, monkeys, squirrels? Would they have relaxed more, given in to siesta more, let the swamps spread in the forest of the sleeping beauty more? Respond please. *"If vines had not sprouted from my body would the Earth been less parched?"* perhaps asked Frida when paitning *Roots*. Respond please. Would the fruits been less conspiratorial to secure? Less sold at premium, more bartered? Knock, knock. Respond please.

Waves quiver rocks

Kisses pout ears

Feet thud hands

As of now, radixes are held up by a woman. Her hand stretches to become the tree rhizomes. One arm up. One down. One burdened. One free to sprout. *Changelings* from *Star Trek* join in and become leaves, stems, branches, sprigs, roots, shoots, soil, manure. The woman clings, clings and clings. *Chipko* woman in the thick. If Earth had not been a mother, would it have been pilferaged?

---

*Bitter Leaf: One of the most popular herbs in Africa, employed also by native Americans to treat various ailments *Roots painting was made by Frida Kahlo in 1943 *Changelings: Alien species in the American science fiction, Star Trek, that went into many versions between 1966–2005 *Chipko: Means to cling to, to stick to. The word was employed in a forest preservation movement which began in India in 1973

Paintings by Madhumita Sinha
Mumbai, India

Madhumita Sinha is an HR professional. She is passionate about poetry, painting, and photography, the three P's of her life that keep her busy. She is a published author of two poetry books, *Heartbeats* and *Bits and pieces of me*. She has contributed to eleven anthologies, out of which three are international anthologies. Madhumita contributes a lot to literary magazines and journals worldwide from time to time. She is a true nature enthusiast, and her poetries are greatly influenced by nature. She lives by the Arabian Sea in Mumbai, India, which is her muse for all three of her passions. Her poems have been described as heart-touching, poignant, and highly sensitive.

Anita became acquainted with Madhumita on Facebook as a fellow poet. Later she learned that Madhumita paints stunning scenes that vividly capture her artistic thoughtfulness and depth to which Anita was immediately drawn. Most of Madhumita's art pieces are abstract while having distinctive elements of realism in them.

The flame of the forest

Flame and escape

I don't watch or read news after eighteen hundred hours. It feels more inhospitable, bleak, stark. During the day I find myself wading with those who died or lost someone to gun violence, murders, accidents, diseases, rapes. I writher, tremble, sometimes stare vacantly into nothingness trying to be them or their families. Why is humanity on a headstand even when blood clots pack tight the reasoning grids? If it's taxing to bring myself home later what about those who were on the news? It's the heart that God could have made differently so that suffering could be painted numb. We could have roamed in corridors of the brain still being innovative, yet our hearts could have been just pumping like many *Datas*. Some would call that surviving, not living. Misguided or not, *Data* too wanted to be human. The other day, after turning off the television, after folding the morning newspaper, after dinner with family, I sat on the balcony overlooking the ocean vistas sipping Baileys on the rocks. Oh, the prim and proper, and luxury of the selected few. Not millionaires by any chance, though still very lucky. We are in the thick of winter yet the grazing of chilly winds on our lanai furniture upon which my body rests, cools my cinching heart. Young herring seagulls were flying towards the South while the older congregated nearer home. I too am aging yet primary colors are still perky and vivid on paper and in my brain synapses. I hurriedly lay flat the morning newspaper and smack my nerves upright and organic. I could decipher the words and sentences still blinking in the background like distraught ambulances, yet I kept my gaze fixated on the forest flame of my basic insignias with enough room between tree trunks for an escape.

*Datas/Data: Data was an android in the television series, Star Trek, The Next Generation

Namaste

Prayer

Its dawn. I've washed, brushed, lit some incense to commence the day. Hands enjoined in *Namaste* close to my core. That is where I must continue to seek. In the channels of conversations threading my conscience. Threads are pure silk betokening a possibility. A promise of not severing easily. Inside I start the day with some yoga. Outside, garbage trucks collect people's daily landfills for fabricating reclaimed land. Planet has more water, less land, more population, less civility. And then we sleep on some of that very reclaimed land. Sometimes it swallows us whole. Sinking chasms don't bother for life. Yes, we sleep on reclaimed land. I also sleep on my reclaimed heart after you pound it flat like a thick piece of meat to cook it better for your taste. Yes, I live in my reclaimed heart as it's still throbbing, composed, pacific, clean, still mine. I took the thick piece of meat out the skillet. Dipped it in a bowl of *Ganga* water and gave it life again. The garbage trucks have left. Little of the foul stench of our messiness trails behind. Sometimes a whiff tries to force itself through open doors, windows. I have trained to breathe in deep *Pranayama* and let out in a hush gently urging stinking whiffs out. As my yoga concludes, I bow in *Namaste* over the incense smoke dancing in the kitchen shadows and urge some blessings towards life.

*Namaste: Traditional way of greeting in India *Ganga: Considered the holiest of rivers in India *Pranayama: Deep breathing exercises

Visual & Mixed Media Art by Michael D. Harris
Georgia, USA

Michael D. Harris is an Associate Professor Emeritus of African American Studies at Emory University. Previously he taught at the University of North Carolina, Morehouse College, and as an adjunct at Duke University, Wellesley College, Spelman College, and was a visiting professor at Dillard University in New Orleans. Prof. Harris is a practicing artist and a long-time member of the artist collective, AfriCOBRA. He has exhibited his work across the United States, in Europe, and in the Caribbean and is represented in many public and private collections. He also has published poetry since he was in his mid-20s, worked as a curator, and taught studio art and art history for 40 years. Currently, Prof. Harris has a book-length manuscript, *Sanctuary: Conjuring an Africana Art Aesthetic*, in production at Duke University Press. His recent book, *Colored Pictures: Race and Visual Representation,* won two national awards. For more on Michael, please visit the website: https://www.michaeldharrisart.com/

Anita became familiar with Michael's terrific mixed-media art when she met Michael almost ten years ago because of professional contacts. She has followed his multi-faceted artwork since then, finding in them a deep sense of history that compels folks to stop and think.

Penance for Oshun, archival digital media, 30" x 22". Oshun is the Yoruba deity of love, motherhood, and feminine energy. She is one of the wives of Shango, the deity of fire and a deified former king or Oba. She is the personal saint of the artist.

Haves and have nots

Remember *Slumdog millionaire*? That's just a movie. There is something infuriating in a group of nobles attempting peace for those who don't have food or water or clothes or a roof or a covered toilet. Aristocrats scoff at those reeking. Pinching their noses, tossing fetid shoes into a bonfire of the indulgent. They keep rambling, advancing. Have nots look hungrily at leftovers, wipe nose grunges off, stand static for hours, and leave their one set of clothing out every night hoping it might rain. The whims of the Haves. The needs of the Have-nots. No just thoughts merging at the confluence of *Alaknanda* and *Bhagirathi* or the *Ohio* and the *Mississippi*. Different strokes for different folks. The snake is flushed. One quarter of the moon is a bride. The veil is polka dotted. My chair is regal. I sewed my own gown. I see *Harriet* and others singing coded spirituals. Felled trees float upstream. Mercury is a fire burning in frozen Jupiter. And then the solitary dove in the harem of the Haves is cuddled, petted, passed from one perfumed bosom to another before "they" decide to let it fly. Let it be free. Other unalike birds watch intently as peace is a name given to one of their step-kind. Any bird can be eaten on costly chinaware with fuddy-duddy sprinkle of seasoning.

*Slumdog Millionaire: Film made in 2008 *Alaknanda and Bhagirathi Rivers: in Devprayag, India *Ohio and Mississippi Rivers: Cairo, Illinois, USA *Harriet: Reference to Harriet Tubman

Patterson Family Quilt

Humdrum of my fabric

Fabric. Material. Cloth. By which name would you want to call me? After chores are done, I mingle with other women in the courtyard. It's an ordinary day as most days need to be. Just a celeste sky. Light, soporific breeze. A no-nonsense stone-mud house. The women feel my style, swoon over the hues I am washed in or the way I have motifs etched over my body and spine. Then they weave me into a kaleidoscope of wondrous contours and senses for humans to wrap themselves. Sometimes, a man complains of an uninterested lover and the women patch in variants of green envy. Sometimes, a woman reveals a diaphanous face of joy ruminating over a love-night, and I'm laced in hues of pinks, reds spilling between dots of burgundy. Sometimes, the weavers' men walk across into the inner rooms giving them lustful glances and a few splashes of dramatic black and purple are intertwined as rejections at the sex hints. The elderly women sitting under the shade of a *Baobab,* noticing the humdrum crisscrossing upon me, make sure to mumble loud enough to stitch in some blue, yellow, brown, grey and relaxed fingerprints, to smuggle in some wisdom and maturity too.

*Baobab: Baobabs are long-lived deciduous, small to large trees with broad trunks and compact crowns, native to Madagascar, Africa, and Australia

Redbone Side-Eye, 48" x 36", on wood panel

What's up?

What's up? Don't ask my young, already tired triangles, squares, some blanks in between as to what's up. Nothing's up, but your preposterous dealt of cards. That you shuffled. That you forced me to cut. That you fabricated in the tin splattered, roof sagging shack you call the man's cave. The chin of the roof of your grouchy belly button. The flying nosily of your booger bear nose hairs. The shimmying to scratchy of your jagged, nefarious toenails. Loud shrieks follow. Mouths blaring come flying from all directions. My young already tired triangles, squares, some blank spaces in between leave my body, ascending high, forming a force field around me. I double up in my nakedness. Yearn for relief. A burst of light and a fuse in your man cave followed by a brash, brassy smash of your foot striking the force field, jacked me from my compelling, captivating reprieve and I stand up with a jolly jump, walking out in *Kintsugi* confidence. My young already tired triangles, squares, some blank spaces in between fixed by gold follow like a long train of a bride's gown inscribing *"what's up"* on the ground.

*Kintsugi: Japanese tradition of repairing broken pottery with powdered gold signifying that missteps, scars, and flaws need to be celebrated, including those of/by people

Quilt Art by Manju Narain
Chicago, Illinois, USA

After moving to the United States from India, Manju, a polyglot and translator, started experimenting with art, fabrics, and quilting. The US offered a lot to a newbie quilt enthusiast. Manju always had a love for patchworking as she grew up seeing her mother make colorful jewel-like Dohars (Hindi for light quilts) for the family. Her mom made Dohars with fabric remnants from dresses she made for her daughters. Manju experiments with designs and materials. Her inventory of quilts includes portraits, modern art, patchwork bed and baby quilts, table runners, etc. She is continuously looking to expand her patchworking repertoire. Manju also continues to work as an interpreter in Hindi, English, and Spanish. Her other interests include sketching, decoupage, alcohol ink art, and mosaic work. Manju has a Master's in the Spanish language, a Bachelor's in Teaching, and a Diploma in Residential Planning. Find her work at: https://www.facebook.com/pg/Quiltomania-483664662057510/posts/
And: https://instagram.com/quiltomania.1?r=nametag

Anita and Manju are childhood friends. They went to the same school in New Delhi, India, and lived in the same locality. In fact, their houses were opposite each other's! Manju's environmentally friendly, very creative and intricate patchwork developed through a methodical approach has deeply impressed Anita.

Tumble in space

Life

My muse is life. Life is my muse. See all the muses of all the people in all the world, in a circle ruminating. Crazy, maybe. Like a boomerang off its tailored path, or a drone revolving like a switchless fan, or me pirouetting like *Sleeping Beauty* in her sleep. Yes, in her sleep, not mine. In mine, sleeping and waking are not tough . . . yet. It ain't like there ain't no water . . . yet. It ain't like there ain't no *roti* . . . yet. It ain't like *Marie Antoinette*'s back from the guillotine, shouting hoarse, *"Let them eat cake."* The world's muse has lost luster though. Like phallic creatures in *Tanguy*'s *The Dark Garden*. Or hens cackling unseen. I just let gratitude fill to the brim as prayers leave my lips repeatedly. Prayers mouthing everyday overlooked words. *"Good night. Good morning. Hello! How are you? Thank you! I am sorry."* Other muses step out of *Maslow*'s triangle and sprint to my side. Water, food, home, and my son who is my home. A romantic love too can be a muse. See, having a muse is not tough. Being one is. Whose muse, am I? What museship do I fill? Ask the connoisseurs of art, or cravers of sunken treasures. Again, and again at the mercy of screams in deep waters. Or sharks. At the center lies the bank's vault. Those that thieves attempt penetrating. Thieves of life. Life that can be a muse. Of sanity. Sanity is life. And life is sanity. Just a simple *khichdi* I remember from my mama's recipes, cooked in slow open pot, sprinkled with fresh ginger bits lightly sautéed in *ghee,* just before serving. My muse I carry all the time. In those gym pants with side pockets, I especially bought for that purpose. Easily reachable like prayer chanting beads. And mostly when I am awake, I see flowers and stars. Some flowers like stars or stars like flowers. Starfish. Vivid, almost illuminating the backdrops of my muse yearnings.

---

*Roti: A round flatbread native to the South Asian subcontinent made from whole wheat flour. *Maslow: Abraham Maslow was an American psychologist who created the triangle of a hierarchy of needs. *Ghee: clarified butter *Yves Tanguy, French surrealist painter, created The Dark Garden in 1928 *Khichdi: A simple comfort food native to the South Asian subcontinent

Quilt by Manju based on a painting by Anju Mathur inspired by Picasso

Muse of biorhythms

The highs and the lows traipse through. Through the blue maze that changes blues. Zig zagging, merrily munching on an apple a day keeps the doctor away. Every angle from where I look, the face is heavily patched. A little lopsided or two despite the apple, and the arctic and sky blue. The chin is crooked, the forehead split yet not wretched. The joker and the jester are bubbly and alive. Their jokes and laughter though sticky as if they'd come straight from a beehive. I see *Hitchcock* befuddled scratching his head, poor man. He thinks the highs and lows have no special mind, soul, heart, or body plan. Forget *Kamasutra*! So, he eyes the escape route for himself. One that was not in his *Birds* movie bookshelf. In and out go the eyes. Not far behind are the goodbyes. The ears are not matching. Seemed the muse meant them for a spanking. The muse the biorhythms had carefully petitioned. Yet I can easily punch in my birthdate and have one daily commissioned. It's a head without a body smiling at us. Painted like shock therapy on a moving bus. *". . . nothing about this place made any sense . . ."* yet cyclic biorhythms are shifting, reactivating, adding new value. Wipe the sweat, seems like there is a breakthrough.

---

*Kamasutra: An ancient Indian Hindu Sanskrit text on sexuality, eroticism, and emotional fulfillment in life said to have been written by Vātsyāyana
*Birds: A 1963 American horror-thriller film produced and directed by Alfred Hitchcock * ". . . nothing about this place made any sense . . ." Part of a line spoken by Thomas from the movie *The Maze Runner*

Graphite Pencil Art by Anthony Gartmond
New Jersey, USA

Anthony Gartmond is a graphite pencil artist, former New Jersey retired prosecutor and attorney. After retirement in 2013 he focused his attention purely on his art and has achieved significant praise and major accolades. His artwork has been successfully exhibited at WBGO Jazz 88.3 in Newark, NJ, Astah's Fine Art Gallery in Maplewood, NJ, Moody Jones Gallery in the Philadelphia, PA metro area, the Montclair Art Museum in Montclair, NJ, and at the celebrated Art in The Atrium exhibition in Morristown, NJ. His work also currently appears on the online gallery of Philadelphia's renowned October Gallery. In addition, Gartmond has been honored with a fine arts award by the Association of Black Women Lawyers, and by the New Jersey State Bar Association, for whom he was the featured artist in the 2021 Black History Month exhibition. In 2021, Anthony received the honor of being inducted to the Hall of Fame in the City of East Orange, NJ. Anthony has a bachelor's degree in Political Science from Rutgers University, and a juris doctor degree from Rutgers Law School.

While Anita met Anthony almost eight years ago, only later she realized what a dazzling artist he was in the medium of graphite pencil drawings. She was instinctively drawn to his art because of its hyperrealism. Anthony's drawings capture iconic and unknown personalities, moments in history, places, and time, with an ethereal aura and a keen eye for attention to detail especially in the play of light and shadows.

I interpret my colorless drink

Pour yourself some scotch. Pour yourself some water. Pour yourself some erudition from the *Tree of Souls,* and I'll listen. Pour yourself some ire, some envy, some conceit, and I'll stare at you enough to freeze you down. Don't be fooled by my *Prada* tailored suit. The devil's been walking at the edges and I'm quite industrial in my taste, interpretive of your musings, including me. Drawings resting against raw, textured, unprepared walls set the tenor. Windows as tall as in airplane hangars alight the ambiance. So, please, pour yourself some scotch. Pour yourself some water. Pour yourself some erudition from the *Tree of Souls,* and I'll listen. Pour yourself some ire, some envy, some conceit, and I'll stare at you enough to freeze you down. I'm a *nyctophile* and aurora. I'm the stream of consciousness and I often sit in vacant chairs in banter with uncountable, undiscovered minted ideas. I ain't got much time. No one got much time. I ain't unique. No one's unique. I ain't above board. No one's above board. Yet this is as interpretive as I can get that when the song returns dragging its overused legs, I'm the one running out hugging, apologizing for the marching orders one too many. I move around, rummaging for some salve, before finding my way back to the main. Friends become acquaintances. Latter just stop being anything. Pandemic could be blamed if you wish, though blaming an illness makes not for a genuine white lie when I still want to be the light's blessing. So, please, pour yourself some scotch. Pour yourself some water. Pour yourself some erudition from the *Tree of Souls,* and I'll listen. Pour yourself some ire, some envy, some conceit, and I'll stare at you enough to freeze you down.

*Tree of Souls: name of the sacred tree for the Na'vi people in the movie Avatar *Prada: A luxury Italian clothing company *Nyctophile: A person who has a special love for the nighttime

Child's game

It ain't a child's game. Ain't a child's game. Not of merry-go-rounds, nor hop scotches, nor the jump ropes, nor the jack-in-the-box kinds. So, please don't point at them. Maybe their reflections like aliens are your skewed perceptions. *E.T.* was kinder. Kids just know how to wait, wait, and wait. Play, play, and play. Chirpy. Carefree. Along with pets who play eye spy around the chirpy playground. Growling now and then, sniffing bottoms, marking pee stations, wagging tails, sprawling in pools, munching on foliage, and cartwheeling on petite windmills. A dog. A cat. A frog. A rabbit. A turtle. A hamster. Children just wait and play. With other children and their shadows, they believe are friends from *Disney* movies. No divisions emerge over tattoos, cars, mansions, each other, or vaccines. All this glamor or sham could be the *Baby's Day Out*. But they still wait. For daddy to return. For mama to return. For the doorknob to turn. Can hear the glee, the squeals, a scene of warmth without need of a lavish fireplace. They aren't playing a game. They aren't like *Games Nations Play* either. No randomness in killings like in big city subway pushes either. Maybe bullying or meanness, sometimes. Some kids. But crude games they do not roll to gross bids. That's what some adults want us to opine as that's what some do.

*E.T.: The Extra-Terrestrial is a 1982 American science fiction film produced and directed by Steven Spielberg *Baby's Day Out: An American comedic movie made in 1994 *Games Nations Play is a book by John Spanier (1995)

Kisses at the espresso bar

All dressed and out. High heels tick-ticking between hide, membrane, cloth. Barely touching, just hinting. So were the shades and lights, and the froths in the cups and the cakes, and the sugars and the creams. Swirling like sips in the dips of the lips and the hips. Seemingly in an animated conversation.

"Some gulp us down too quickly forcing us to burn their tongues, throats. Some give long respites forcing us to cool down leaving no pleasure in the sips. And her, she seems a bit tense, a bit lost, her attention span is low. She coils us in the cups long enough for us to snooze. Then with a glance at the server for the check, she dumps us like peeled bananas left on a counter too long. She doesn't know we are the best of best espresso of old Connaught Place cafes, leaving a craving for your touch, your kisses, innately inside . . ."

The sheen and the glean in the coffee machine remain unseen as counters, spic and span, take center stage. Stage is immaculate, swept, dusted. Raw. And knowledge, wisdom, enigma, passion is brewed in one, as the counters gesture her to perk up. She holds her fingers tersely, glancing here and there, her lipstick leaving tales and tails. *"I really want to be cool today. As cool as Oppenheim's imaginative fur cup. Or shall I say hot. Or absurd, as some say?"* She whispers to someone on the phone. Animated conversations are nudging each other breathlessly. The sips in the dips in the lips and the hips are ready as she hurries out blowing kisses at the froths in the cups, and the cakes, and the sugars, and the creams.

---

*Connaught Place: A central shopping area in New Delhi * Fur-covered cup: A reference to the art by Méret Oppenheim (1936), one of the first few women surrealist artists

Two wells

From where I see, the bail goes deeper yet I don't hear the splash. It slithers up. Not recoiling though. She's dry. No one can tell. And then she's not dry. That too no one can tell. One well within another. Both try to satisfy thirst. Lush, emerald circling them. Upside and downside. In the verdant, prolific meadows of life, I can walk naked feet. Or just naked. Hopping from stones to stones. The frogs hoot. Grass blades to grass blades murmur. No one's watching except the sky seeming to be a helping hand. No dismal, obscure clouds scrutinize in antipathy. The flat outside is better to lay on and enjoy a blissful winter afternoon sun. The curved interiors are risky yet tempting. Both are quite lonesome. Not lonely. Abundant yet denied. Welcoming like an afternoon coquettishly lingering for some sugar from winsome evening. The needy hang around, restlessly, fingers tapping. Let's forget the wells and succulent, ambrosial surroundings for a moment. Focus on being menopausal early. Quite enjoying this kind of bloody freedom. It's my world, I'm letting you in. So, drink away till I say no, and don't touch anything that isn't meant for you. Not even the sculpted makeup of the *joker* in *Batman* can convince me of anything possibly good. Water is rare these days. So rare, contaminations are not even boiled or filtered. Therefore, come, nod, and leave on time. Don't forget to promise to return one day. It might be your final lie. I'll fend ignorance and faith. The bail, the water, the thirst may be more amenable then.

*Joker in Batman movie, 1989

Jazz vocalist

Smooth jazz flows through me, soft, tempting, experimenting like an alchemist searching, yearning, transforming lost souls into solid again. There's an ocean flowing through the club where I'm performing, and *The Middle Passage* is ignited red. All around ancestors are wailing. Unnerving screams are unable to break the chains. Burnt rose buds fly around bawling my saga wondering how they'd survive infancy. You, and you, and you, or even you, may not fully get it. The sweet fragrance and the tears fusing in my veins. Don't ask me whose fault it is. Delve your arms into your belly for that gut of yours. Pull it out. Shake it. Awake it. Ask it. Outside it's raining saxophones and plethora of hums, echoes, reverberations, and silence. The last is louder than all. Some wood, some mast, some gold, some skin, some souls. The other day I went on a fancy cruise to where the slave ships tore through alien waters far, far away from home. Saxophones were enthralling there. The top deck was brilliant, mopped clean. Though, tearful. Though, queasy. And many stood watching the heartbeats of the ocean in satin and silk dresses and velvet tuxedos singing midnight extravaganzas. It's raining dead people. Love and hearth are confused. My body, your touch. Strings of music notes hold us together.

*The Middle Passage: Lasting roughly eighty days, the distance between West Africa and the New World across the Atlantic Ocean transporting slaves in tightly packed ships, with barely enough room to lay down or any place to defecate. It's said approximately 14% to 15% of the about 12–13 million enslaved people did not survive this journey

My soul sits at the edge of Arlington and Washington DC

Quietly awaiting my return. Arms crossed, kinda slouched, in grass blades drenched to their nucleus, at the corner of where Arlington and DC shake hands. Puddles around me. Tiny pools of hope glistening, swaying, grooving with drops that fall incessantly. Cities are strange creatures. Souls of millions smacked upon each other like cardboard boxes in windowless *gowdans* without anything to color. That's why, perhaps, hues of big cities can be fossil-like, gloomy, depressing at times, like tones of despair at funerals. Yet, sometimes, cities when wet are like butter I love spreading on a slice of untoasted bread. Dotted with sugar granules. Or creamy like caramel evenings. Or smooth like my pointed suede pastel pumps. Petrichor that comes from ground admixed with cloud spray uplifts me. I see outlines of bodies rejoicing, clothes palpitating, enticing, despite their clinginess. New Delhi monsoon rains join me as I walk through Arlington and DC rain. That's why synesthesia's intriguing. Misty merging of senses like myriad worlds in *My Dress Hangs there*. Many umbrellas had pitched tents around my soul. Some had my parent's faces on them. Some of friends. Some of school mates with whom I blurted puzzlements of adolescence. Some of my son with whom I drove through Arlington streets building new lives. *I will always love you* by *Whitney* was humming itself to warm bittersweet memories in a mason jar filled with tiny lights, iridescent like fireflies waiting for my soul. At the edge of Arlington and Washington DC, its face full of salty smudges.

*Gowdan: A Hindi word denoting a warehouse *My Dress Hangs There was painted by Frida Kahlo in 1933 *I will always love you: Song by Whitney Houston released in 1992

Can surrealism be a bench?

It sure can. It's imagination after all. Hurriedly people cross the bridge. It's not too full. Still, I hear the steps and the words bouncing like tennis balls against steel railings. Everything on the bridge glows like gold dust. The sky too. The lights and the air too. Pixie dust. Magical. Arousing. The bench is gold leafed. I create hearts, drawing in eyes, nose, smiling lips. And like a snow fairy I sketch circles in fine amber powder. Slowly the finger lines stand up. Nearby mod-fancy-tech machines prepare to create new humans to relax on the bench. Canoodling, arguing, people watching. Is that right? Was *Dolly,* right? Soon the bridge becomes crowded and perky. Embellished in all its might. Nuts and bolts dancing on their belly and back. Words, steps are less audible. Expressions more animated. Extraordinary and ordinary. Can't tell if that's the commencing of a celebration or a hiatus before all hell breaks loose. The world is a stage and *Ellison*'s invisible man keeps possibilities alive in his bunker not too far away. Streets glow like *Chirico*'s 1914. The bench is discreet, inobtrusive now. I see *disquieting muses* sitting on it, mum and stiff. Squabbles of the real housewives and househusbands have receded.

*Dolly: First sheep to be cloned in 1995 *Ellison: Reference to Ralph Ellison and his novel, The Invisible Man *Girogio de Chirico, a surrealist painter made his, Mystery and Melancholy of a Street in 1914 and The Disquieting Muses in 1917

Not really like *Mona Lisa*

Like *Mona Lisa,* I carry secrets. Who doesn't? I'm not smiling like Lisa, though. I'm the one behind the camera. Focused, with penetrating *kohl*-glazed eyes and painted, inquisitive lips, hungry for that world famous iconic-to-be captured. Forgotten legends seek rejoinders, sometimes reposts. The slight bend at the shoulders, tilt at the head, squinting at the eye, all mutter about what I'm hauling. Boding burdens and then some. Cigarette smoking is injurious to health. So, I quit. Want and want, I want to share injustices and wrongs but not their ghastly smothering. I leave those to the media outlets. Instead, I intend clicking emotions. Yes, those very feelings, sentiments, that history is not complete without. Overlooked in the concrete finality of death, ignorance, misreporting, subjectivity. Whose *Time on the Cross,* was it? Choosing sage and moss like *Amrita's Sumair,* so I'd be close to Mother Earth, I sit pretty on a baroque settee and the marsh flows around me, claret flowers on the marsh. He said he'd be home early. Wedding anniversary is not to be missed. I appear in saddened sepia now. The lonely wife, or the ignored woman photographer? Chose the one that validates you, for I'll depend on God to take care of me. The food now is icy. Candles now pulverized. Winter now relentless. And I don't feel like changing clothes now. Thickened and darkened is the marsh now. Without the high of achievement, every day, like a satisfying orgasm, my collapsing at night would not be worthwhile. Like my first love that vanished in Philadelphia. His kisses, still hot on my lips. Shoot, it's already morning. I have endless selfies awaiting development.

*Kohl: Ancient eye cosmetic still used in South Asia *Time on the Cross: A 1974 book by Robert Fogel and Stanley L. Engerman *Amrita Sher Gil: An Indian-Hungarian avant-garde artist who painted Sumair in 1936

Tears can come anytime

Child: I see you. I see you, a soft bundle of heaven. A melodious dreamland in a tender wrap. One I imagined you'd be handed to me in for the first time. First time when you and I bonded . . . birthed flesh to flesh, gene to gene, soul to soul. That delicate wrap. One that you later lay snugly tucked in a bassinet, wide-eyed, cooing, seeking me for sustenance, cleaning, connecting. I fly in and out of waterfalls and effervescences nestling with you in budding jasmines, surrounded by soft flute hums of Hermit thrush birds, and temple bells as I wonder why heaven came down and said, *"Hello, mom, I'm baby Krishna. Here just for you."* What did I do to deserve you? Aging, sagacious gurus join me as we cry our hearts out.

Parents: I see you. I see you both, in separate hospital rooms, on separate hospital beds, at separate times. No sound from either. Just silent, unsuccessful attempts to pull out feeding tubes or bear the pain. I didn't need airplanes to get to you. Yet when you both flew away, a pea each in two pods, I wasn't in either. I ran from one to the other, yet you remained just a bit ahead, just a bit too far for me to catch. To beseech. To beg to return. And then, *Antarctic* emptiness came and sat next to me as if I needed it more. When you and your dreams fragmented, your tears became mine.

Lover: I see him. I see him as he walked around with ease in his unclothed skin, his muscled frame still chiseled and wanting. I lost my hesitations soon enough as my nakedness still revealed an hourglass figure. As night somersaulted into dawn, his baritone kissed my husky. And blooming plants in his living room seemed to be whispering agreeably, as did the smiling exercise machines. Nature and nurture had trained us to enjoy another love after a long drought. Tears finally filled the driest riverbeds in the *Atacama Desert.*

*Krishna is a major God in Hinduism and considered an incarnation of Lord Vishnu *Antarctica: US Antarctica participant guide calls it the emptiest place on earth *Atacama Desert: It's in Chile, and it's said that some riverbeds there have been dry for 120,000 years

Singing and lingering seven-year itches

Tabby: could be from *Friends* that *Phoebe* sang about. Ain't that smelly like in the song. Kind of aloof. Kind of bored. Done the catwalk for seven years now. Beneath her stairs darken and the room eclipses deliberately. She looks a bit cold. Maybe she sat in the winter, too long? Maybe she got washed in chiffon shawls of the haze? Maybe she heard the owls hooting, foretelling drizzles? Maybe she got stuck in the stiff collar the sun wore? Maybe she crossed her own path? Maybe we all are a wee bit superstitious. Humans don't have many human friends. And so, she sings, *"Quiet woman, quiet woman, where do you hail from? Quiet woman, quiet woman, what are you hiding from?"*

Model: was a wee bit late for a photo shoot. Silk stockings enfolded her, far too long. The corset was being testy, far too long. Cashmere stoles weren't the right color. It's been raining cats outside for seven years now. The dogs had gone for a run instead. Sprinting up the stairs, she spotted the cat passing over her with a know all face. Unwinding, she sat, prim and proper, arched back and sang, *"Funny cat, funny cat, what are you thinking now? Funny cat, funny cat, what are you going to eat now?"*

Wife: bought some fancy lingerie from *Saks Fifth Avenue,* not too long ago. To surprise her man when he'd return home. Travels a bit much these days. Carries no luggage. His seven-year-old messenger bag rests sulking on a side of the bedroom. Her smalls were restless, so she wore them, calming and stroking the folds. And then sitting deftly, perched on the floating stairs, fingertips pirouetting around the steps, she sang, *"Scooting cat, scooting cat, do you've a word about my man? Scooting cat, scooting cat, have heard about my man?"*

*Friends: An American television sitcom created by David Crane and Marta Kauffman aired on NBC from 1994 to 2004. Phoebe is one of the main three women characters in the series. *Saks Fifth Avenue: An American luxury store founded in 1867

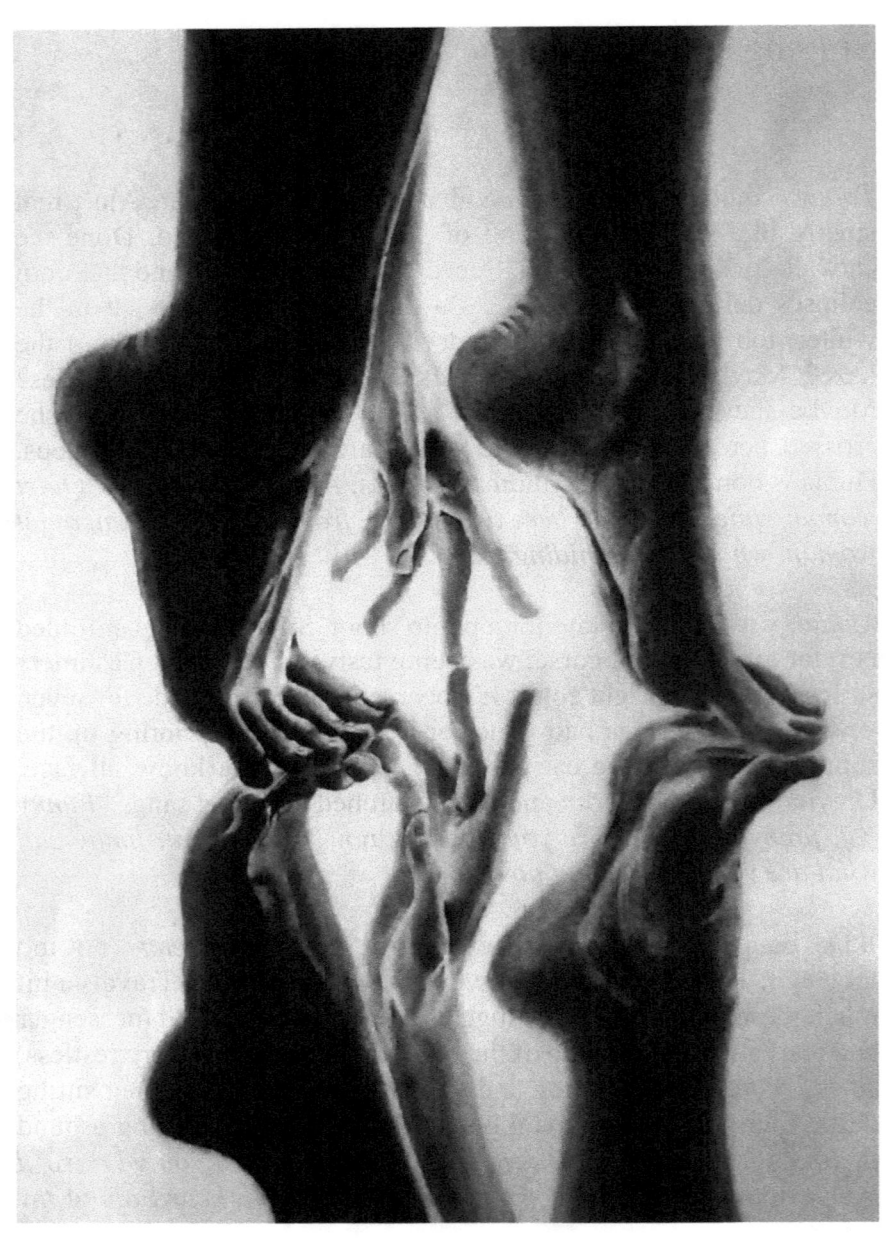

Whispers

My hands tiptoe to the tip of your toes. Don't somersault. Just linger. Stride softly. In the distance, I hear a moan. Loud enough to measure on the *Richter* scale. The machine on the table is going berserk. Many coryphées are circling with crème de la crème, hand-picked *Merlots, Malbecs, Madeiras,* and a skyscraper speaks in strapping notes like early morning intonations. Canals of fresh gladiolus flow by, garlands of *rajanigandha* tread water, and a few drops of *Oud* rise to the surface. All within arm's reach. Should I dare even breathe? As I slide off the skyscraper, steel and my *Scent of a Dream* collide. Touch points behind ears, on wrists, between thighs, beneath my navel are invigorated. *"Stop cussing,"* you say. *"My curses are speckled with sugar, honey."* There's a loud crash as glass shatters.

*Merlot, Malbec, Madeira: Kinds of red wines *Rajanigandha: Hindi name for Tuberose flower *Oud: Perfume from agarwood bark *Scent of a Dream: A Charlotte Tilbury fragrance that is supposed to be mind-blowing in its sensuality. Its mystic notes include lemon, peach and black pepper, jasmine, frankincense, tuberose and violet, plus psychoactive pheromone base notes of fire tree, Iso E Super, patchouli and ambroxan

About the Author

Anita Nahal, Ph.D., CDP is an Indian American poet, flash fictionist, children's writer, professor, and D&I consultant. She teaches at the University of the District of Columbia, Washington DC. Previously she has worked at Howard University, George Mason University, Chicago School of Professional Psychology-DC campus, Rider University, Smithsonian National Museum of African American History and Culture, Sri Venkateswara College, University of Delhi, India, Indira Gandhi National Open University, India, and Kamala Nehru College, University of Delhi, India.

Nahal has authored thirteen creative books: four of poetry, one of flash fiction, four for children, and four edited anthologies. Anita's poems and flash fiction can be found in journals in the US, UK, Asia, and Australia. Her poems are also housed at Stanford University's Digital Humanities Initiative. Anita's writings focus on the intersection of race, gender, immigration, socioeconomic status, and other issues that create bias and injustice. She was a finalist in 2022 and 2021 respectively for the Cats poetry and Women's artist contests at *The Ekphrastic Review* and received an honorable mention in the 2016 Concretewolf Chapbook contest. Her third poetry book, *What's wrong with us Kali women* (Kelsay Books, 2021), was nominated by Cyril Dabydeen, Guyanese Indian Canadian & Ottawa poet laureate emeritus & novelist, as the best poetry book for 2021 for British Ars Notoria. It's also compulsory reading in an elective course on Multicultural Society at Utrecht University, The Netherlands. Anita is the daughter of Sahitya Akademi award-winning Indian novelist Chaman Nahal and educationist Sudarshna Nahal. Anita resides in the US. Her family includes her son, daughter-in-law, and golden doodle girl.

More on her at: https://anitanahal.wixsite.com/anitanahal

www.ingramcontent.com/pod-product-compliance
Lightning Source LLC
Chambersburg PA
CBHW060839190426
43197CB00040B/2702